COMPLET
of Preschool

Thinking Kids®
An imprint of Carson Dellosa Education
Greensboro, NC

Thinking Kids®
Carson Dellosa Education
PO Box 35665
Greensboro, NC 27425 USA

ISBN 978-1-4838-6236-1

01-067211151

Dear Parents, Caregivers, and Educators,

The *Complete Book* series provides young learners an exciting and dynamic way to learn the basic skills essential to learning success. This vivid workbook will guide your student step-by-step through a variety of engaging and developmentally appropriate activities in basic concepts, reading, math, language arts, writing, and fine motor skills.

The *Complete Book of Preschool* is designed to be used with an adult's support. Your student will gain the most when you work together through the activities. Below are a few suggestions to help make the most of your learning time together:

- Read the directions aloud. Move your finger under the words as your child watches. As you come to words he or she recognizes, encourage your student to read along.
- Explain the activities in terms your student understands. Talk about the pictures and activities. These conversations will both strengthen your student's confidence and build important language skills.
- Provide support and encouragement to your student. Work with your student at a pace that is comfortable for him or her. End your learning time when your student shows signs of tiring.

To find other learning materials that will interest your young learner and encourage school success, visit www.carsondellosa.com

TABLE OF CONTENTS

Basic Skills

I Said Red

Color the pictures **red**.

Now, trace the word **red**.

Hello, yellow!

Color the pictures yellow.

Now, trace the word yellow.

True Blue

Color the pictures **blue**.

Now, trace the word **blue**.

The Green Scene

Color the pictures green.

Now, trace the word green.

Name _____

What About Orange?

Color the pictures orange.

Now, trace the word orange.

Think Pink!

Color the pictures pink.

Now, trace the word pink.

Purple Power

Color the pictures **purple**.

Now, trace the word **purple**.

Brown Is All Round!

Color the pictures **brown**.

Now, trace the word **brown**.

Name _____

Bonjour Black

Color the pictures **black**.

Now, trace the word **black**.

White in Sight

Color the pictures white.

Now, trace the word white.

Name _____

Circle Time

This is a **circle**. Trace the shape.

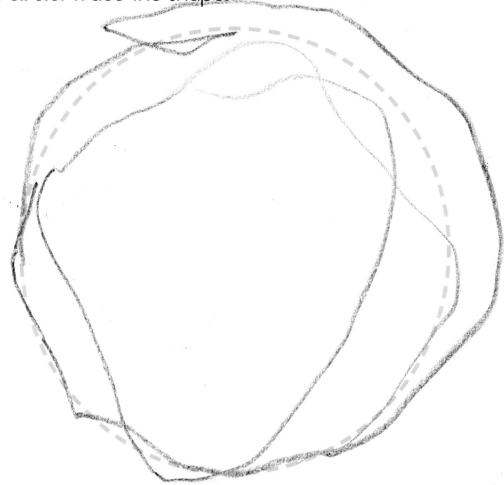

Trace the word.

This picture has **circles** in it. Trace the circles.

Earth

Mars

Jupiter

Saturn

Name _____

Fair and Square

This is a **square**. Trace the shape.

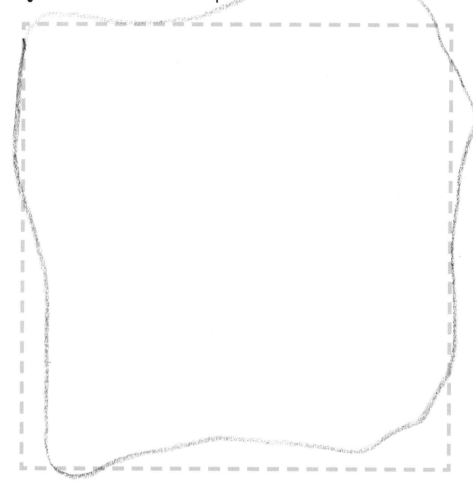

Trace the word.

square

This picture has **squares** in it. Trace the squares.

Triangle Tricks

This is a **triangle**. Trace the shape.

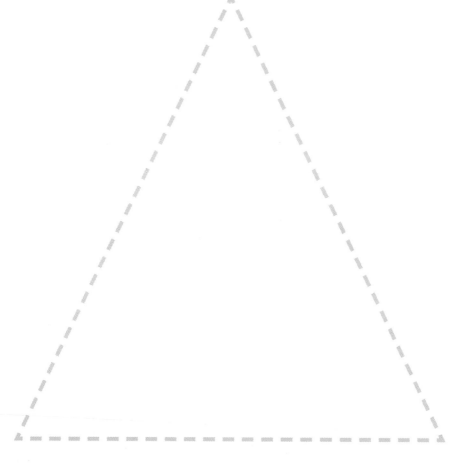

Trace the word.

triangle

This picture has **triangles** in it. Trace the triangles.

Rectangle Tango

This is a **rectangle**. Trace the shape.

Trace the word.

rectangle

This picture has **rectangles** in it. Trace the rectangles.

Only Ovals

This is an **oval**. Trace the shape.

Trace the word.

oval

This picture has **ovals** in it. Trace the ovals.

Rebellious Rhombuses

This is a **rhombus**. Trace the shape.

Trace the word.

This picture has **rhombuses** in it. Trace the rhombuses.

Review Shapes

Draw a line to match each shape on the left to the same shape on the right.

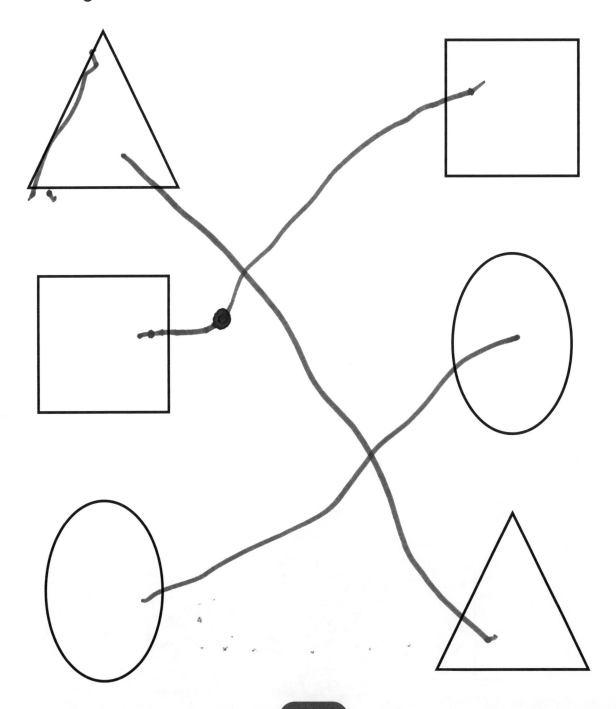

Review Shapes

Draw a line to match each shape on the left to a picture with the same shape on the right.

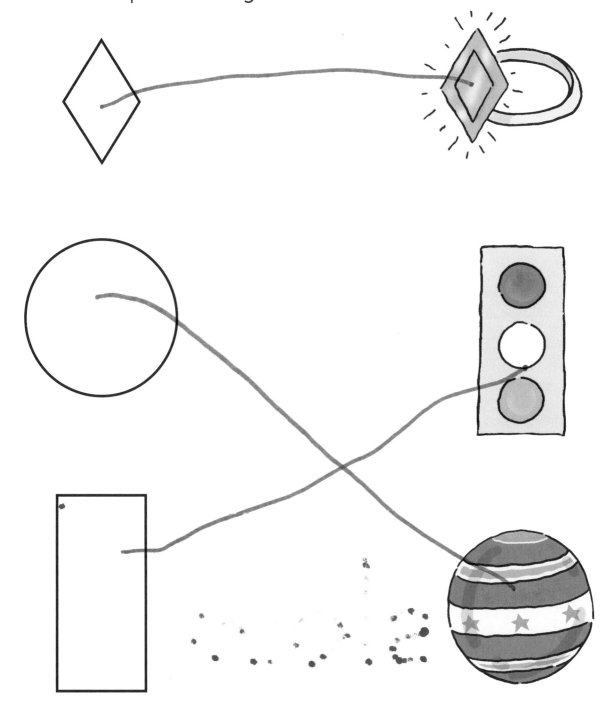

The Tortoise and the Hare

Look at the picture. Trace the word.

slow

Look at the picture. Trace the word.

fast

Doghouse Day

Look at the picture. Trace the word.

Look at the picture. Trace the word.

out

I Scream, You Scream

Look at the picture. Trace the word.

Look at the picture. Trace the word.

sad

Sun and Snow

Look at the picture. Trace the word.

Look at the picture. Trace the word.

cold

Writing Readiness

Hungry Critters

Help the cat get to the milk. Follow the arrow to trace a path to the milk.

Help the rabbit get to the carrot. Follow the arrow to trace a path to the carrot.

Caterpillar Crawl

Trace the lines from top to bottom to make each caterpillar's legs.

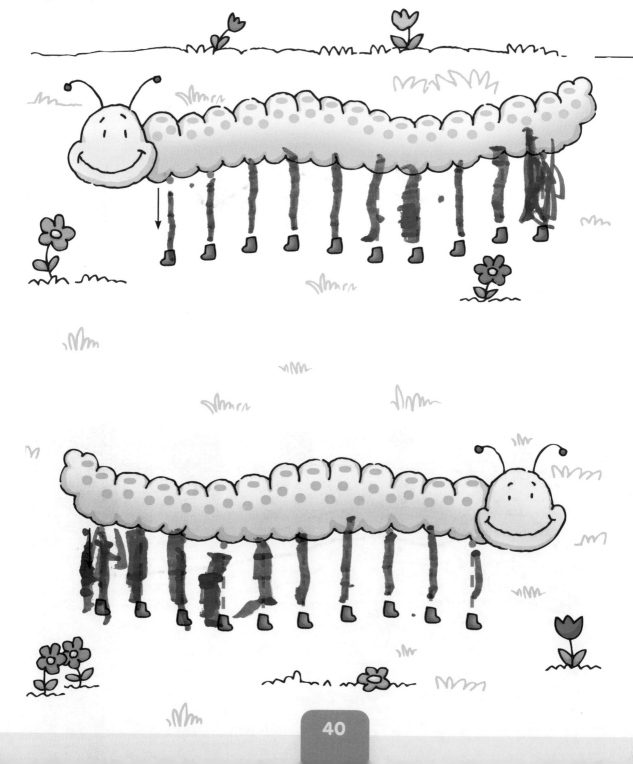

Slip and Slide!

Help the children go down the slides. Trace the lines from top to bottom.

Busy Bees

Trace each bee's path from left to right.

Now, draw this bee's path on your own.

Reading Readiness

Name _____

Fun with Aa

Trace UPPERCASE **A**.

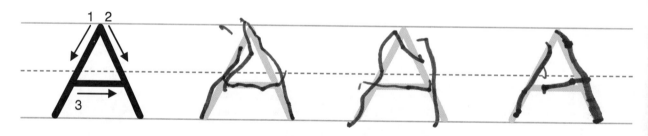

Now, write UPPERCASE **A**.

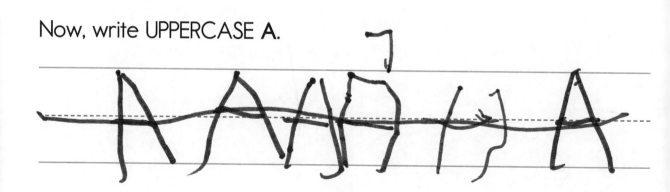

Trace lowercase **a**.

Now, write lowercase **a**.

Name _____

Color Me A

Say the names of the pictures. Color each picture that begins with the sound of **Aa**.

Up the Apple Tree

Color the **A**'s red. Color the **a**'s green. Color the other letters

Name _____

Fun with Bb

Trace UPPERCASE **B**.

Now, write UPPERCASE **B**.

_____

- - - - - - - - - - - - - - - - - - -

_____

Trace lowercase **b**.

Now, write lowercase **b**.

Name _____

Match It!

Draw a line from each letter **b** to a picture that begins with that sound.

b

b

b

Hungry for Honey

Help the bear get to the honey. Use a crayon to trace the **Bb** path to the honey tree.

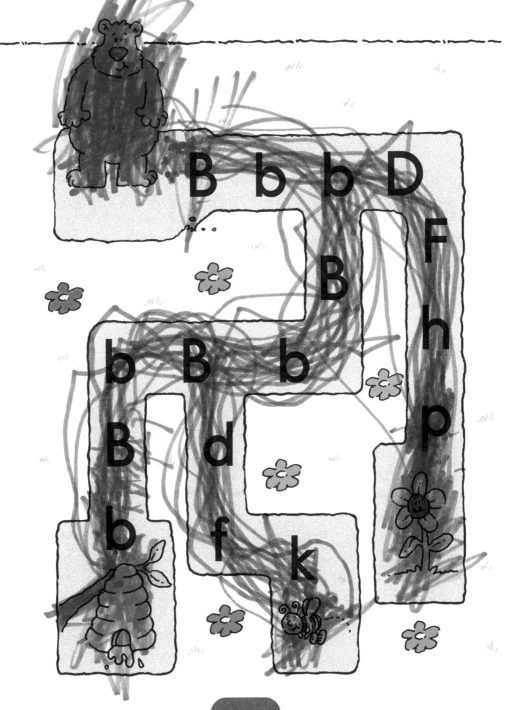

Name _____

Fun with Cc

Trace UPPERCASE **C**.

Now, write UPPERCASE **C**.

Trace lowercase **c**.

 C   C   C   C   C

Now, write lowercase **c**.

Name _____

Color Me C

Say the names of the pictures. Color each picture that begins with the sound of **Cc**.

Name _____

Cats in Clothes!

Look at the patterns on the cats' sweaters. Draw a line between the cats with matching **Cc** patterns on their sweaters.

Name _____

Letter Review

Look at the letter each person is holding. Circle the same letter in each box.

Letter Review

Look at the letter each person is holding. Circle the same letter in each box.

Fun with Dd

Trace UPPERCASE **D**.

Now, write UPPERCASE **D**.

Trace lowercase **d**.

Now, write lowercase **d**.

Dino Days

Trace the letter **D** on the dinosaur's plates.

Dolphin Dives

Help the dolphin jump through the rings. Color the rings that have the letter **D** or **d** in them.

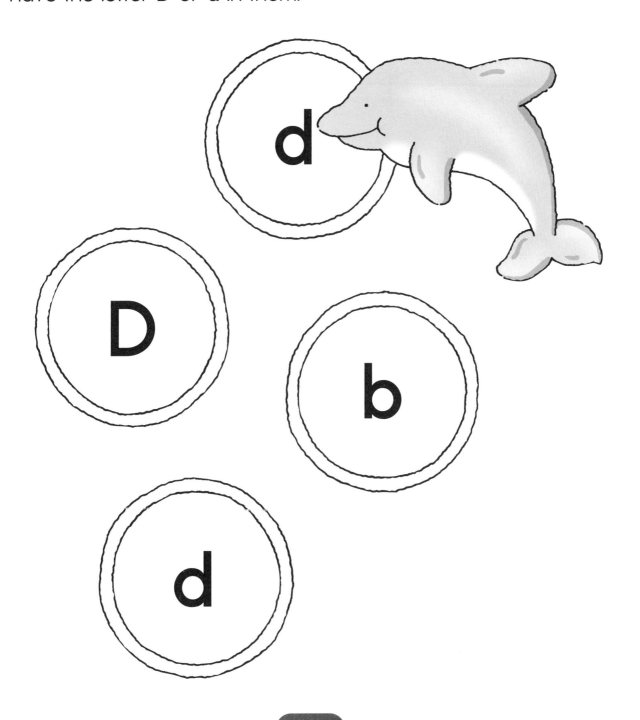

Fun with Ee

Trace UPPERCASE **E**.

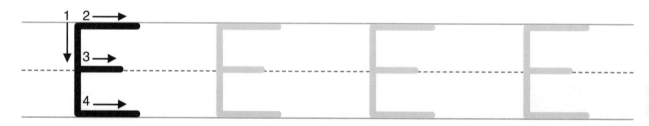

Now, write UPPERCASE **E**.

Trace lowercase **e**.

  e   e   e   e   e

Now, write lowercase **e**.

Name _____

Color Me E

Say the names of the pictures. Color each picture that begins with the sound of **Ee**.

Egg-cellent!

Trace the letter **E** or **e** on each egg.

Name _____

Footprint Fun

Help the baby elephant get to its mother. Color the footprints with **E** or **e** on them.

Letter Review

Trace the letters on the caterpillar. Write the missing letters where they belong.

Fun with Ff

Trace UPPERCASE **F**.

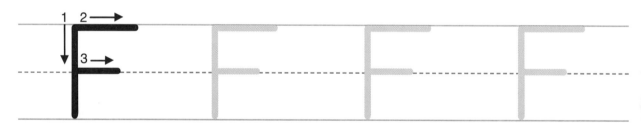

Now, write UPPERCASE **F**.

Trace lowercase **f**.

Now, write lowercase **f**.

Name _____

Color Me F

Say the names of the pictures. Color each picture that begins with the sound of **Ff**.

Gone Fishing

Color the fish in the fish bowl. Color the **F** fish orange. Color the **f** fish green. Color the other fish with a color you like.

Name _____

Fun with Gg

Trace UPPERCASE **G**.

Now, write UPPERCASE **G**.

_____

- - - - - - - - - - - - - -

_____

Trace lowercase **g**.

 g g g g g g

Now, write lowercase **g**.

Let's Start with G

Write the letter **g** under the pictures that begin with the sound of **g**.

_____   _____

_____   _____

_____   _____

Name _____

Duck, Duck, Goose

Color to find the hidden picture. Color the spaces with **G** yellow. Color the spaces with **g** brown.

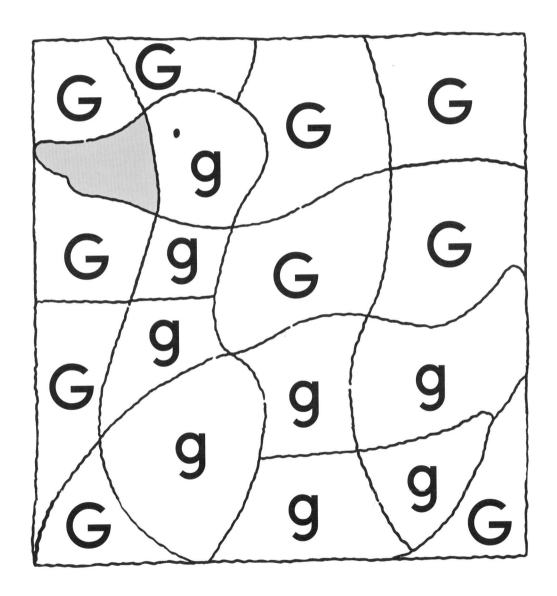

What did you find? _____

Name _____

Letter Review

Draw a line from the UPPERCASE letter on each kite to the lowercase letter that matches.

Name _____

Letter Review

Draw a line from the UPPERCASE letter on each kite to the lowercase letter that matches.

Name _____

Fun with Hh

Trace UPPERCASE **H.**

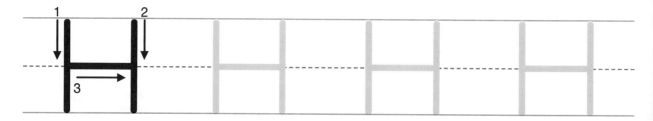

Now, write UPPERCASE **H.**

_____

- - - - - - - - - - - - - - - - - -

_____

Trace lowercase **h.**

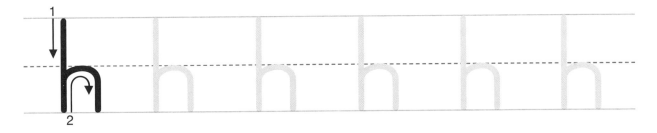

Now, write lowercase **h.**

_____

- - - - - - - - - - - - - - - - - - -

_____

Name _____

Hats Off!

Color to find the hidden picture. Color the spaces with **H** blue.
Color the spaces with **h** brown.

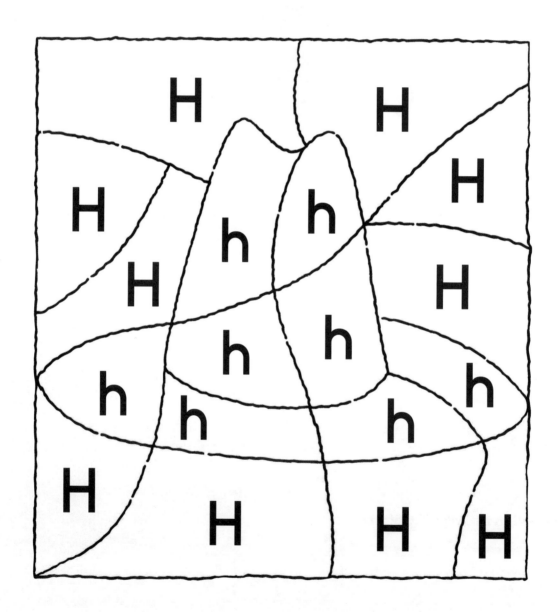

What did you find?_____

Hay Is for Horses

Help the horse get to the hay. Say the names of the pictures. Follow the path with pictures that begin with the sound of **Hh**.

Fun with Ii

Trace UPPERCASE **I**.

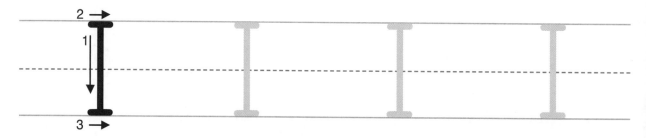

Now, write UPPERCASE **I**.

Trace lowercase **i**.

Now, write lowercase **i**.

Color Me I

Say the names of the pictures. Color each picture that begins with the sound of **Ii**.

Ice Is Nice

Help build the igloo. Trace the letters **I** and **i** below.

Name _____

Inch by Inch

Help the inchworm get to the flower. Circle the letters **I** and **i**.

Letter Review

Trace the letters on the teddy bears. Write the missing letters where they belong.

Name _____

Fun with Jj

Trace UPPERCASE **J**.

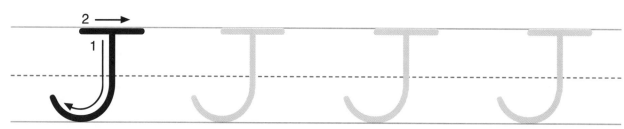

Now, write UPPERCASE **J**.

Trace lowercase j.

Now, write lowercase j.

Name _____

Color Me Jj

Say the names of the pictures. Color each picture that begins with the sound of **Jj**.

Flying High

Jim has a ticket for a ride. Color to find the hidden picture. Color the spaces with **J** or **j** blue. Color the other spaces gray.

What will Jim ride in?_____

Fun with Kk

Trace UPPERCASE **K.**

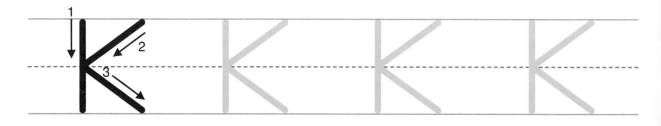

Now, write UPPERCASE **K.**

Trace lowercase **k**.

Now, write lowercase **k**.

Color Me K

Say the names of the pictures. Color each picture that begins with the sound of **Kk**.

Locked Out!

Look at the letters on each key and lock. Draw a line between the keys and locks with matching letters.

Name _____

Go Fly a Kite

Say the names of the pictures on the kites. If a picture begins with the **Kk** sound, draw a kite string from the kite to the child's hand.

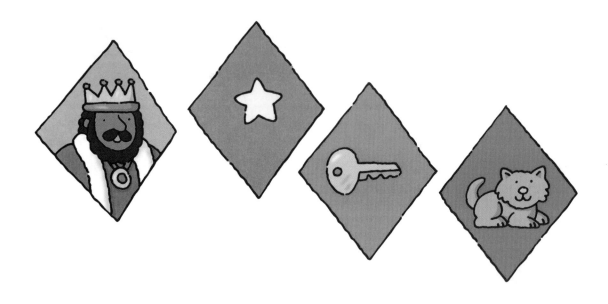

Letter Review

Draw a line from each UPPERCASE letter to its matching lowercase letter.

Name _____

Fun with Ll

Trace UPPERCASE **L**.

Now, write UPPERCASE **L**.

_____

_____

Trace lowercase l.

Now, write lowercase l.

Name _____

Color Me L

Say the names of the pictures. Color each picture that begins with the sound of **Ll**.

Up the Ladder

Climb the ladder by coloring the pictures that begin with the sound of **Ll**.

Fun with Mm

Trace UPPERCASE **M.**

Now, write UPPERCASE **M.**

_____

- - - - - - - - - - - - - - - -

_____

Trace lowercase **m**.

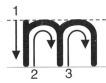

Now, write lowercase **m**.

Name _____

Say Cheese!

Color to find the hidden picture. Color the spaces with **M** gray. Color the spaces with **m** yellow. Color the other spaces with a color you like.

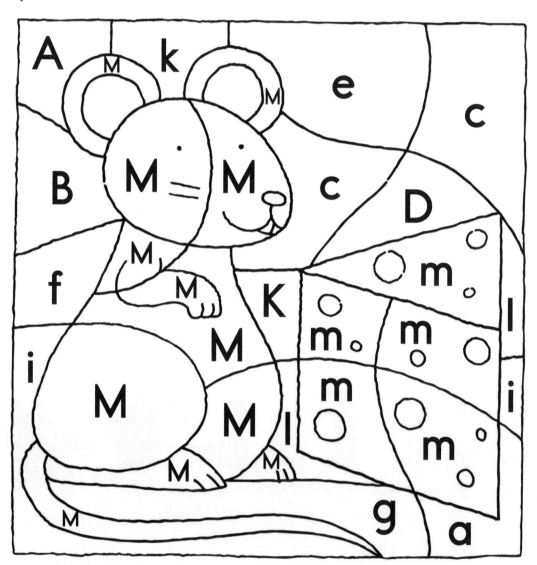

What did you find?_____

Mouse on the Move

Help the mouse get to the cheese. Say the name of each picture. Follow the path of pictures that begin with the sound of **Mm**.

Name _____

Fun with Nn

Trace UPPERCASE **N**.

Now, write UPPERCASE **N**.

Trace lowercase **n**.

 n n n n n

Now, write lowercase **n**.

Name _____

Color Me N

Say the names of the pictures. Color each picture that begins with the sound of **Nn**.

Match It!

Draw a line from the letters **Nn** to the pictures that begin with the sound of **Nn**.

Nn

Nn

Nn

Name _____

Fun with Oo

Trace UPPERCASE O.

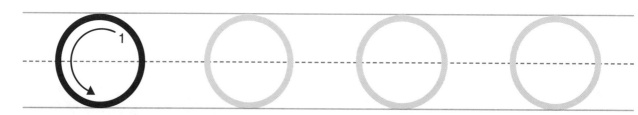

Now, write UPPERCASE O.

Trace lowercase **o**.

Now, write lowercase **o**.

Name _____

Color Me O

Say the names of the pictures. Color each picture that begins with the sound of **Oo**.

Under the Sea

What did the octopus see on the ocean floor? Color the spaces with **O** or **o** blue. Color the other spaces **brown**.

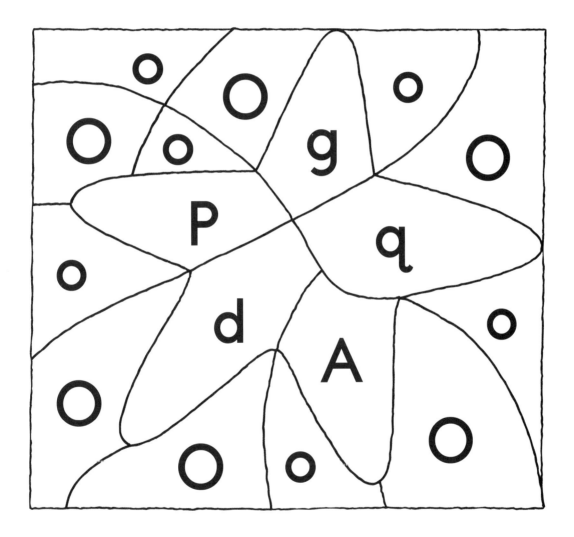

What did the octopus see? _____

113

Name _____

Fun with Pp

Trace UPPERCASE **P**.

Now, write UPPERCASE **P**.

Trace lowercase **p**.

Now, write lowercase **p**.

Color Me P

Say the names of the pictures. Color each picture that begins with the sound of **Pp**.

Party Time!

Cut out the party hats with **P** or **p**. Glue them on the children's heads.

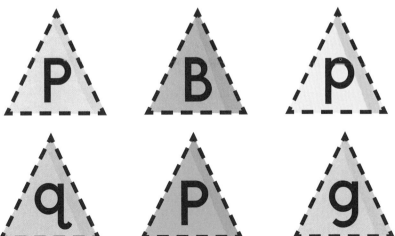

This page is blank for the cutting activity
on the opposite side.

Letter Review

Connect the dots as you say the alphabet from **A** to **P**. Then, color the picture.

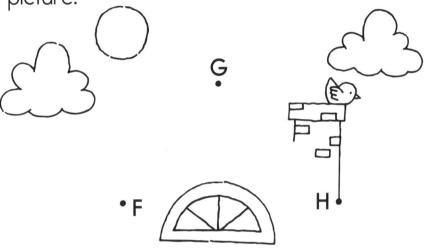

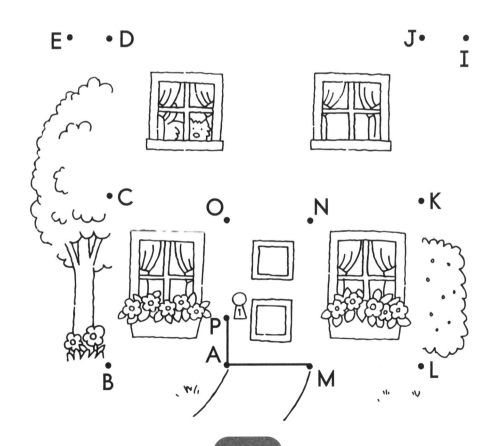

Name _____

Fun with Qq

Trace UPPERCASE **Q**.

Now, write UPPERCASE **Q**.

Trace lowercase **q**.

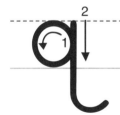

Now, write lowercase **q**.

Name _____

Color Me Q

Say the names of the pictures. Color each picture that begins with the sound of **Qq**.

Colorful Quilts

Color the quilt. Color the squares with **Q** green. Color the squares with **q** pink.

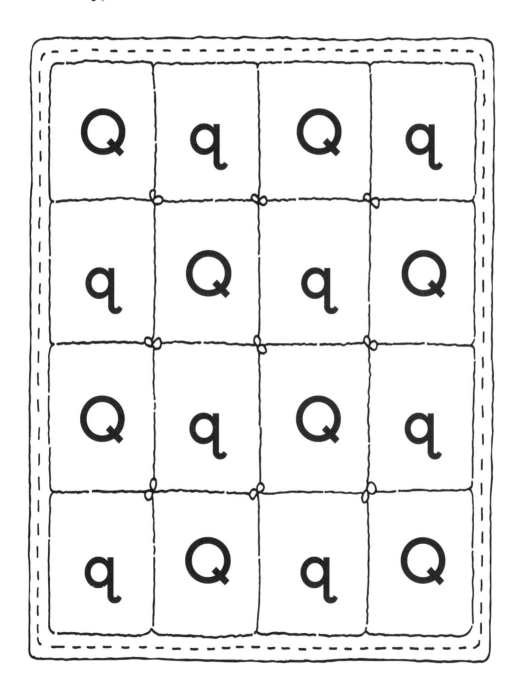

Name _____

Fun with Rr

Trace UPPERCASE **R**.

Now, write UPPERCASE **R**.

_____

- - - - - - - - - - - - - - - - - - - -

_____

Trace lowercase **r**.

Now, write lowercase **r**.

Name _____

Color Me R

Say the names of the pictures. Color each picture that begins with the sound of **Rr**.

Match It!

Draw a line from each **Rr** to an animal whose name begins with the sound of **Rr**.

Rr

Rr

Rr

Fun with Ss

Trace UPPERCASE **S**.

  S   S   S

Now, write UPPERCASE **S**.

Trace lowercase **s.**

 s   s   s   s   s

Now, write lowercase **s.**

Color Me S

Say the names of the pictures. Color each picture that begins with the sound of **Ss**.

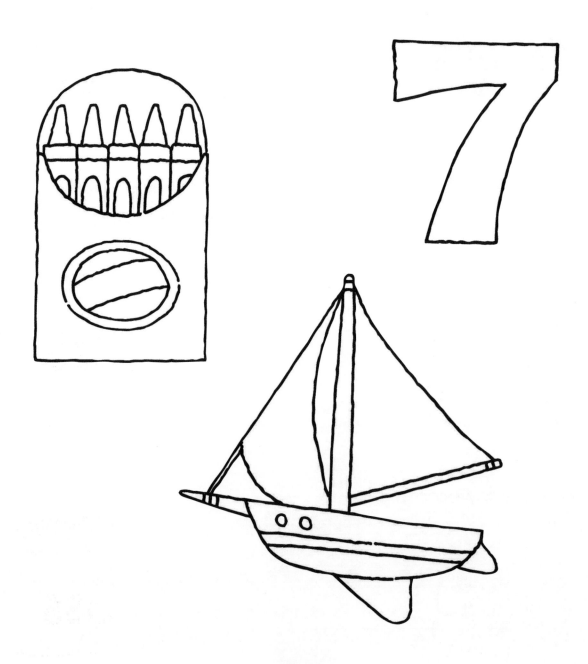

Match It!

Look at the letter patterns on the shirts and shorts. Draw a line from each shirt to the pair of shorts with the same letter pattern.

Fun with Tt

Trace UPPERCASE **T**.

Now, write UPPERCASE **T**.

Trace lowercase t.

Now, write lowercase t.

_____

- - - - - - - - - - - - - - - - - - -

_____

Name _____

Color Me T

Say the names of the pictures. Color each picture that begins with the sound of **Tt**.

Take a Hike!

Help Taylor and her mom get to the tent for their campout.
Follow the path of pictures that begin with the sound of **Tt**.

Name _____

Letter Review

Trace the letters on the bocks. Write the missing letters where they belong below and on page 137.

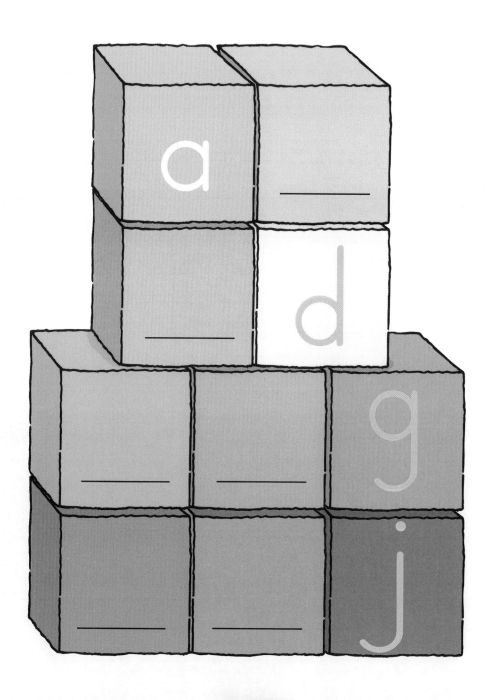

Letter Review

Name _____

Fun with Uu

Trace UPPERCASE **U**.

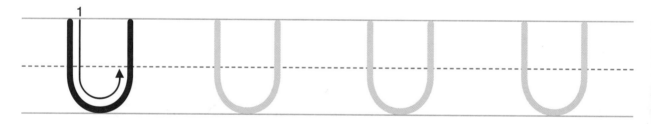

Now, write UPPERCASE **U**.

Trace lowercase **u**.

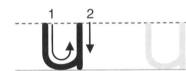

Now, write lowercase **u**.

Color Me U

Say the names of the pictures. Color each picture that begins with the sound of **Uu**.

Let's Rocket!

Blast off to the Moon! Trace the **Uu** letter path to send the rocket up into outer space.

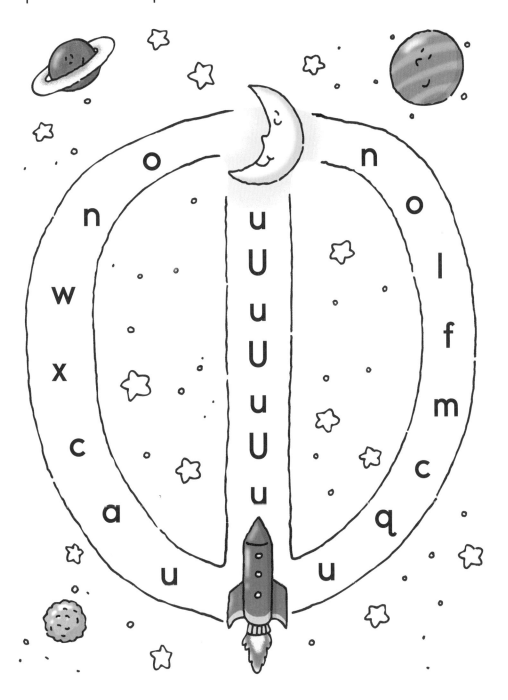

Name _____

Fun with Vv

Trace UPPERCASE **V**.

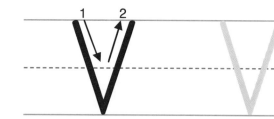

Now, write UPPERCASE **V**.

Trace lowercase **v**.

Now, write lowercase **v**.

Name _____

Color Me V

Say the names of the pictures. Color each picture that begins with the sound of Vv.

Match It!

Draw a line from each **Vv** to a picture that begins with the sound of **Vv**.

Name _____

Fun with Ww

Trace UPPERCASE **W**.

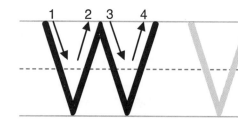

Now, write UPPERCASE **W**.

Trace lowercase **w**.

Now, write lowercase **w**.

Name _____

Color Me W

Say the names of the pictures. Color each picture that begins with the sound of **Ww**.

Windy Weather

Find the things in the picture that begin with the sound of **Ww**.
Then, circle them.

Name _____

Letter Review

Help feed the hungry walruses. Draw a line from each UPPERCASE letter to its matching lowercase letter.

Letter Review

Connect the dots as you say the alphabet from **A** to **W**. Then, color the picture.

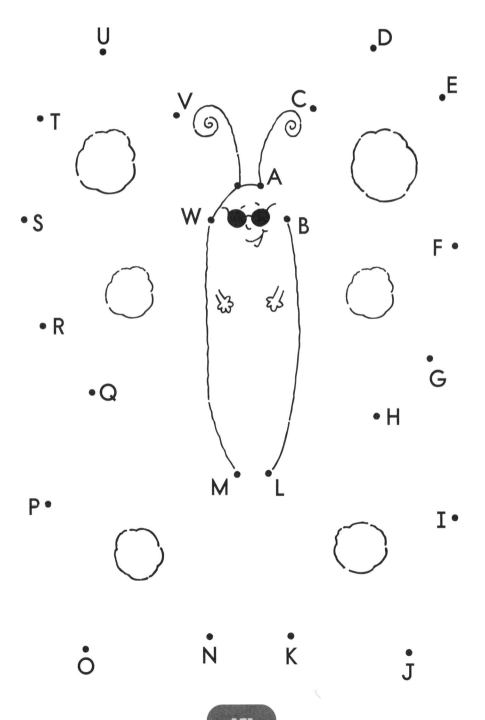

Fun with Xx

Trace UPPERCASE **X**.

Now, write UPPERCASE **X**.

_____

- -

_____

Trace lowercase **x**.

  X   X   X   X   X

Now, write lowercase **x**.

Name _____

Color Me X

Say the names of the pictures. Color each picture that begins with the sound of **Xx**.

X Marks the Spot

Say the names of the pictures below. Then, trace the **x** to complete each word.

fo x

bo x

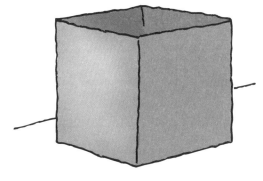

o x

Fun with Yy

Trace UPPERCASE **Y**.

Now, write UPPERCASE **Y**.

Trace lowercase y.

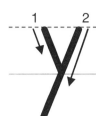 y   y   y   y   y

Now, write lowercase y.

Name _____

Color Me Y

Say the names of the pictures. Color each picture that begins with the sound of **Yy**.

Wild About Y

Color to find the hidden picture. Color the spaces with **Y** yellow.
Color the other spaces orange.

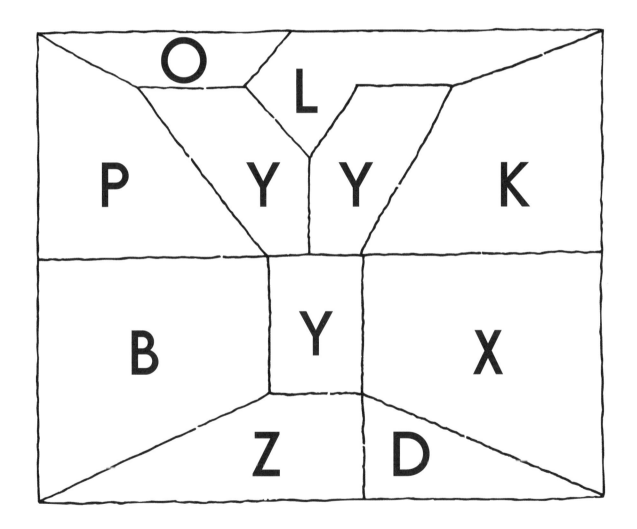

What did you find? _____

Fun with Zz

Trace UPPERCASE **Z**.

Now, write UPPERCASE **Z**.

_____

_____

_____

Trace lowercase **z**.

Now, write lowercase **z**.

Name _____

Color Me Z

Say the names of the pictures. Color each picture that begins with the sound of **Zz**.

Zip It!

These zippers need zipper pulls. Cut out the pictures below that begin with **Zz**. Then, glue them on the zipper pulls.

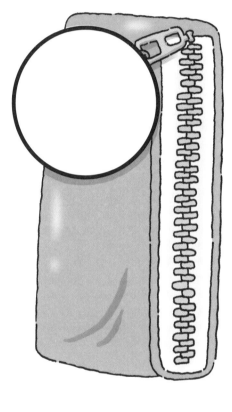
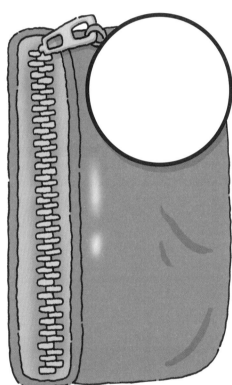

This page is blank for the cutting activity
on the opposite side.

Letter Review

Cut out the letter cards below and on page 167. Match the UPPER- and lowercase letters.

This page is blank for the cutting activity
on the opposite side.

Letter Review

This page is blank for the cutting activity
on the opposite side.

Sound Off!

Look at each picture below. Circle the sound each picture begins with. Then, color the pictures.

s n p

d g b

Name _____

Sound Off!

Look at the pictures in each group. Color the picture that has the same beginning sound as the picture in the circle.

Sound Off!

Look at the pictures in each group. Color the two pictures in each group that begin with the same sound.

Sound Off!

Draw a line from each letter to the picture that begins with that sound.

Rhyme Time

Look at the pictures in each group. Color the picture that rhymes with the picture in the circle.

Name _____

Rhyme Time

Look at the pictures below. Draw lines to match the rhyming pictures.

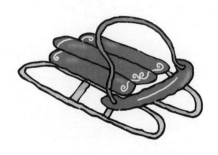

Math Readiness

Counting on 0

Trace the number **0**.

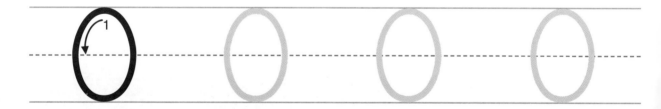

Now, write the number **0**.

Zero

Trace the word **zero**.

zero   zero

Now, write the word **zero**.

Fun with 1

Trace the number 1.

Now, write the number 1.

One

Trace the word **one**.

one   one

Now, write the word **one**.

Name _____

1 • One

Circle **1** picture in each box. Then, write the number **1** on the line in each box.

1 • One

Draw a line to match each number 1 to one thing.

1

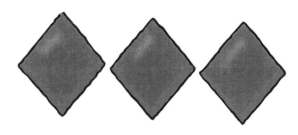

1

1

Time for 2

Trace the number **2.**

Now, write the number **2.**

Two

Trace the word **two**.

two two

Now, write the word **two**.

2 •• Two

Draw a line to match each number **2** to a group of **2** things.

2

2

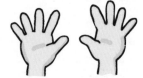

2

2 •• Two

Color to find something that comes in twos. Color the spaces with **2** _____. Color the spaces with **1** blue.

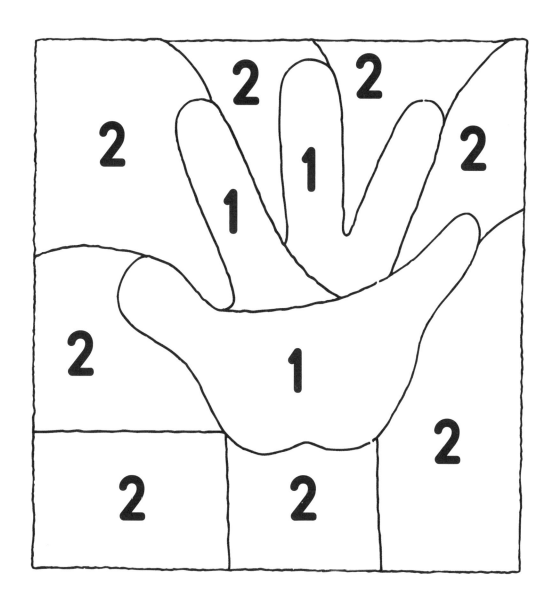

What did you find?_____

3 and Me

Trace the number **3**.

Now, write the number **3**.

Three

Trace the word **three**.

three three

Now, write the word **three**.

3 ••• Three

Draw shapes that complete each pattern of **3**.

3 ••• Three

Draw pictures so there are **3** things in each box. Then, write a **3** on the line in each box.

Take a Ride with 4

Trace the number 4.

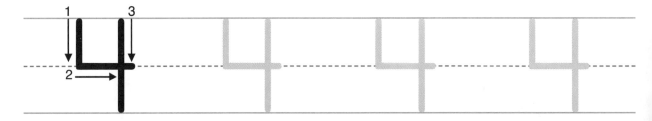

Now, write the number 4.

Four

Trace the word **four**.

four   four

Now, write the word **four**.

4 •••• Four

Count the flowers in each group. Circle the number that tells how many there are.

2   3   4

2   3   4

2   3   4

4 •••• Four

Draw **4** flowers in the vase.

High 5!

Trace the number **5**.

Now, write the number **5**.

_____

- - - - - - - - - - - - - - - - - - - -

_____

Five

Trace the word **five**.

five five

Now, write the word **five**.

5 ●●●●● Five

Count the shapes in each box. Draw more so that each box has **5** shapes in it. Write **5** on each line.

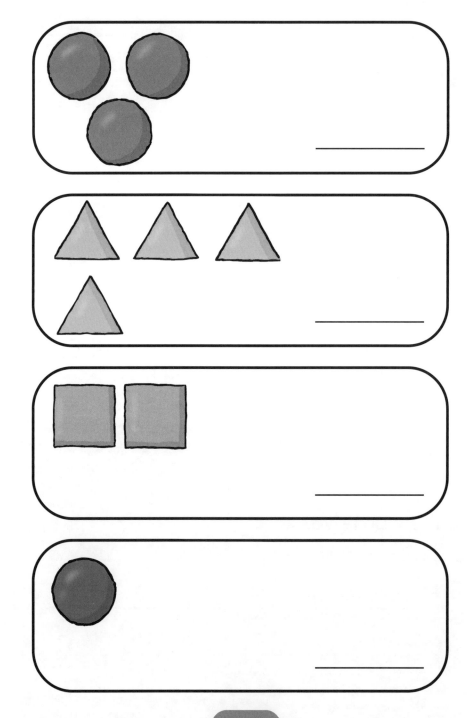

5 ●●●●● Five

Count the shapes. Then, color and decorate the butterfly.

How many ◯s? _____

How many △s? _____

How many ▢s? _____

Name _____

Review 1–5

Count the fish in each group. Write the number that tells how many there are.

Review 1–5

Trace and write the missing numbers below.

1 2 3 4 5

4 5

_____ _____ _____ _____ _____

1

_____ _____ _____ _____ _____

Super 6

Trace the number **6**.

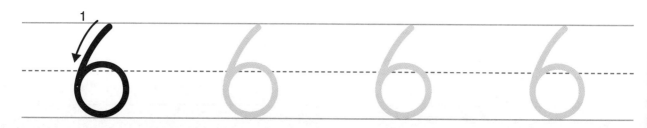

Now, write the number **6**.

Six

Trace the word **six**.

six   six

Now, write the word **six**.

Name _____

6 ⣿ Six

Circle **6** things in each box. Write the number **6** on each line.

_____

_____

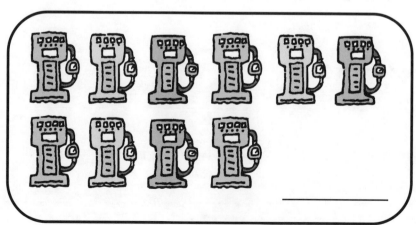

_____

6 ⣿ Six

Help the car get to the gas pump. Use a crayon to follow the path of **6**'s.

Name _____

7 Times the Fun

Trace the number **7**.

Now, write the number **7**.

Seven

Trace the word **seven**.

seven seven

Now, write the word **seven**.

7 ∷∷∙ Seven

Count the peanuts in each box. Write the number that tells how many there are.

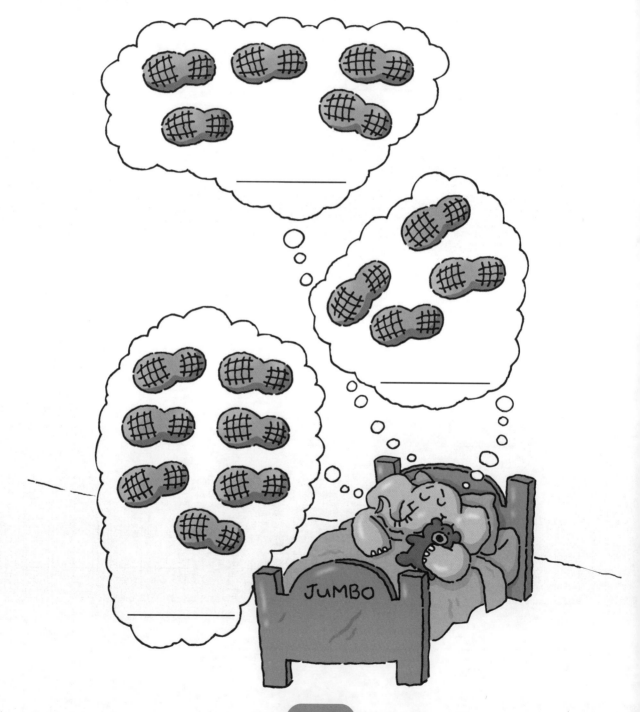

7 ⬤⬤⬤⬤⬤⬤⬤ Seven

Add some toppings to the pizza. Draw **7** pieces of pepperoni.
Draw **7** mushrooms.

Name _____

8 Is Great!

Trace the number **8**.

Now, write the number **8**.

Eight

Trace the word **eight**.

eight   eight

Now, write the word **eight**.

8 ••••••• Eight

Draw a line from each basket to the tree with the same number of apples.

8 :::: Eight

Count and circle **8** legs on each caterpillar.

9 Is Fine

Trace the number **9**.

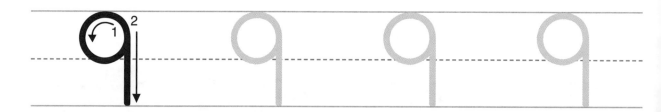

Now, write the number **9**.

Nine

Trace the word **nine**.

nine   nine

Now, write the word **nine**.

Name _____

9 Nine

Circle **9** bugs in each group.

9 Nine

Draw **9** black dots on the ladybug's back.

Top 10

Trace the number **10**.

Now, write the number **10**.

Ten

Trace the word **ten**.

ten   ten

Now, write the word **ten**.

Name _____

10 ●●●●● ●●●●● Ten

Draw **10** leaves on the branches for the caterpillar to eat.

10 ⣿⣿ Ten

Follow the directions to color the butterfly. Color **5** dots **red**.
Color **3** dots **blue**. Color **2** dots orange.

Count the dots on the butterfly.
How many are there altogether? _____

Name _____

Review 6–10

Count the number of dots on each hat. Write the number on the line.

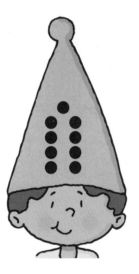

_____   _____

_____   _____

Review 6–10

Connect the dots from **1** to **10** to find a circus treat. Then, color the picture.

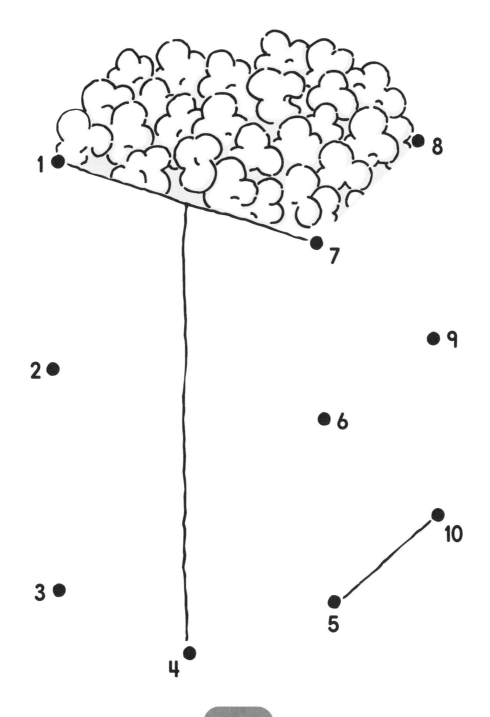

ANSWER KEY

Page 6

Page 7

Page 8

Page 9

Page 10

Page 11

Purple Power
Color the pictures purple.

Now, trace the word purple.

purple

Page 12

Brown Is All Round!
Color the pictures brown.

Now, trace the word brown.
brown

Page 13

Bonjour Black
Color the pictures **black**.

Now, trace the word **black**.
black

Page 14

White in Sight
Color the pictures white.

Now, trace the word white.
white

Page 15

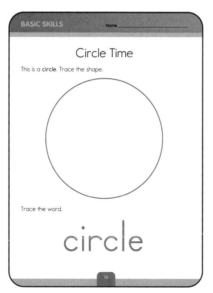

Circle Time
This is a **circle**. Trace the shape.

Trace the word.
circle

Page 16

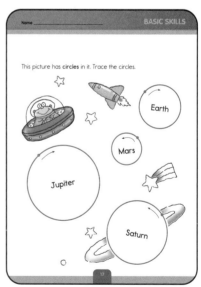

This picture has **circles** in it. Trace the circles.

Earth

Mars

Jupiter

Saturn

Page 17

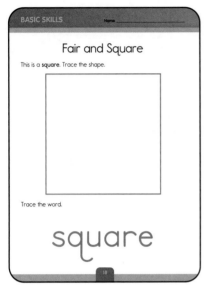

Page 18

Page 19

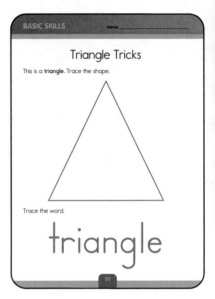

Page 20

Page 21

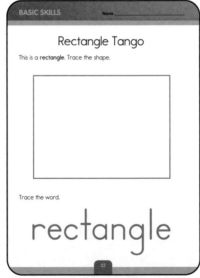

Page 22

Page 23

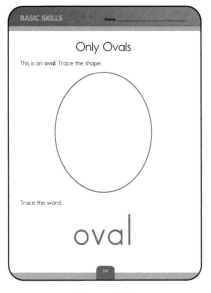

Page 24

Page 25

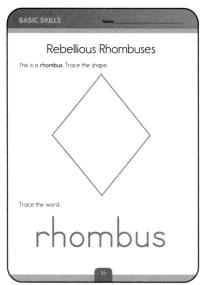

Page 26

Page 27

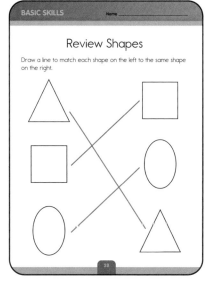

Page 28

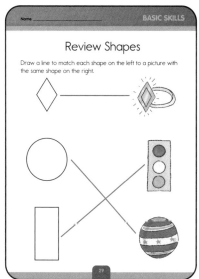

Page 29

ANSWER KEY

Page 30

Page 31

Page 32

Page 33

Page 34

Page 35

Page 36

Page 37

Page 39

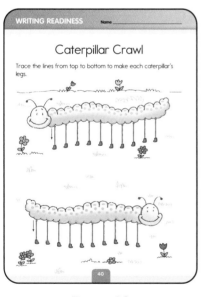

Page 40

Page 41

Page 42

Page 44

Page 45

Page 46

Page 47

Page 48

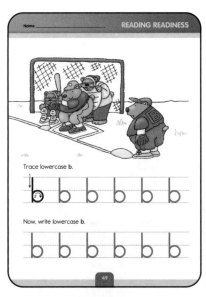

Page 49

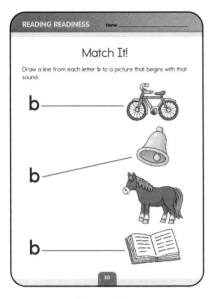

Page 50

Page 51

Page 52

Page 53

Page 54

Page 55

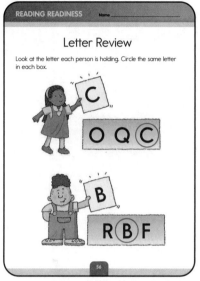

Letter Review

Look at the letter each person is holding. Circle the same letter in each box.

Page 56

Letter Review

Look at the letter each person is holding. Circle the same letter in each box.

Page 57

Fun with Dd

Trace UPPERCASE D.

Now, write UPPERCASE D.

Page 58

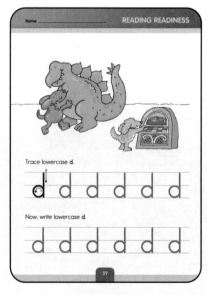

Trace lowercase d.

Now, write lowercase d.

Page 59

Dino Days

Trace the letter D on the dinosaur's plates.

Page 60

Dolphin Dives

Help the dolphin jump through the rings. Color the rings that have the letter D or d in them.

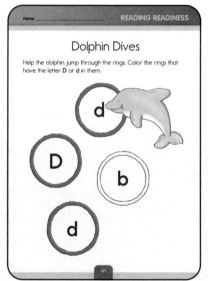

Page 61

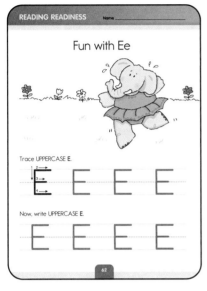

Page 62

Page 63

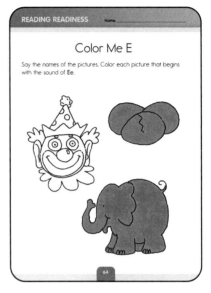

Page 64

Page 65

Page 66

Page 67

Page 68

Page 69

Page 70

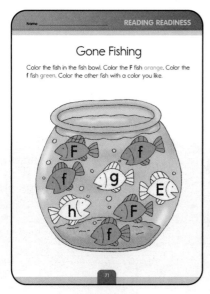

Page 71

Page 72

Page 73

Page 74

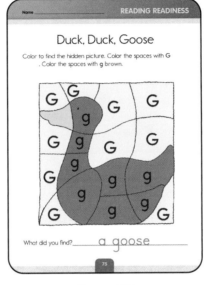

Page 75

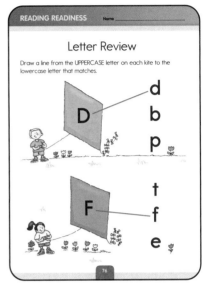

Page 76

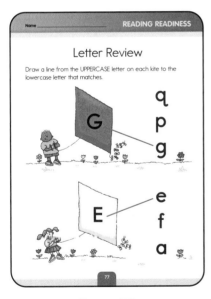

Page 77

Page 78

Page 79

Page 80

Page 81

Page 82

Page 83

Page 84

Page 85

ANSWER KEY

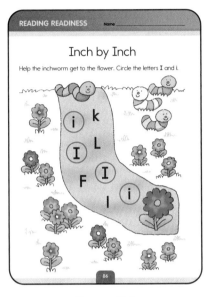

Page 86

Page 87

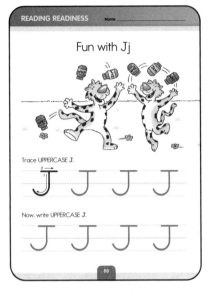

Page 88

Page 89

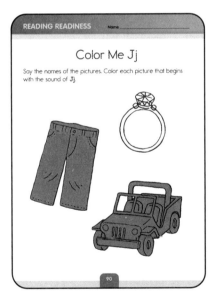

Page 90

Page 91

235

Page 92

Page 93

Page 94

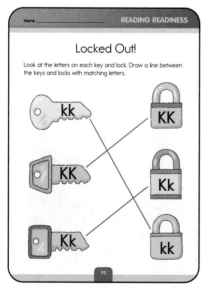

Page 95

Page 96

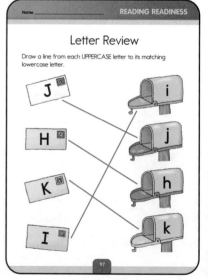

Page 97

Page 98

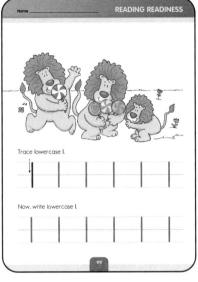

Page 99

Page 100

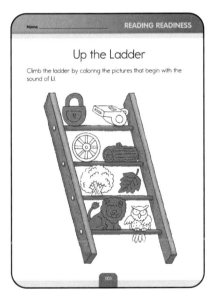

Page 101

Page 102

Page 103

ANSWER KEY

Page 104

Page 105

Page 106

Page 107

Page 108

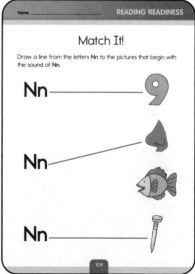

Page 109

ANSWER KEY

Page 110

Page 111

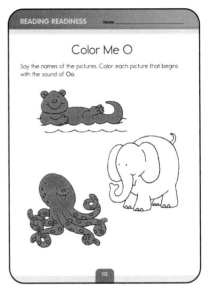

Page 112

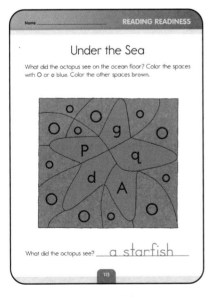

Page 113

Page 114

Page 115

Page 116

Page 117

Page 119

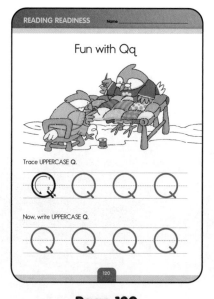

Page 120

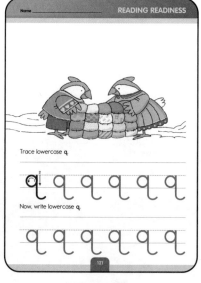

Page 121

Page 122

Page 123

Page 124

Page 125

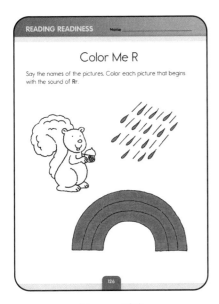

Page 126

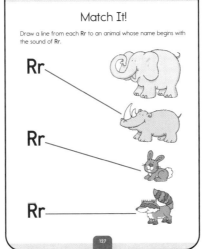

Page 127

Page 128

Page 129

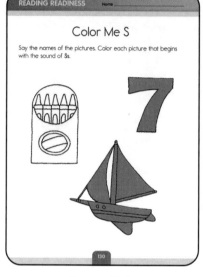

Page 130

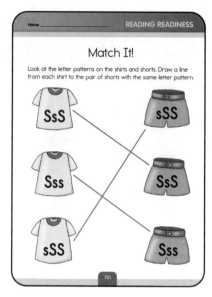

Page 131

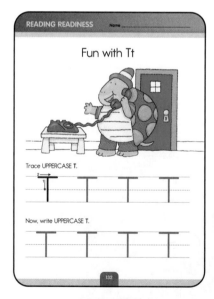

Page 132

Page 133

Page 134

Take a Hike!

Help Taylor and her mom get to the tent for their campout. Follow the path of pictures that begin with the sound of Tt.

Page 135

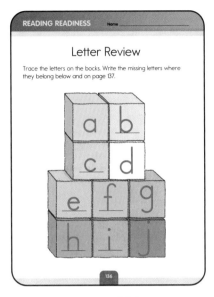

Letter Review

Trace the letters on the bocks. Write the missing letters where they belong below and on page 137.

Page 136

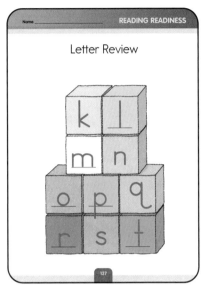

Letter Review

Page 137

Fun with Uu

Trace UPPERCASE U.

Now, write UPPERCASE U.

Page 138

Fun with Uu

Trace lowercase u.

Now, write lowercase u.

Page 139

Color Me U

Say the names of the pictures. Color each picture that begins with the sound of Uu.

Page 140

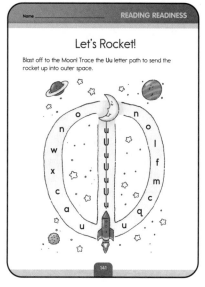

Page 141

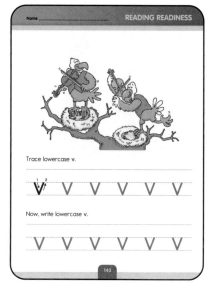

Page 142

Page 143

Page 144

Page 145

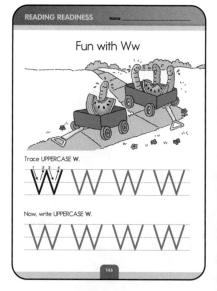

Page 146

Page 147

Page 148

Page 149

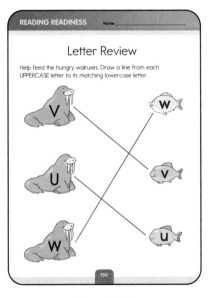

Page 150

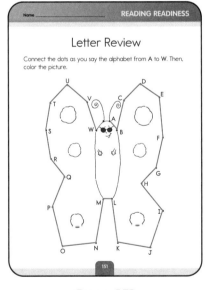

Page 151

Page 152

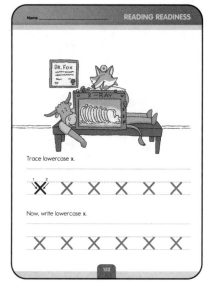

Page 153

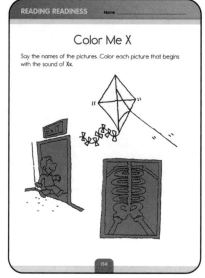

Page 154

Page 155

Page 156

Page 157

Page 158

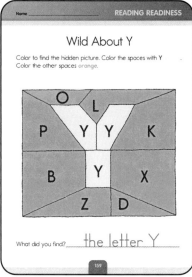

Page 159

Page 160

Page 161

Page 162

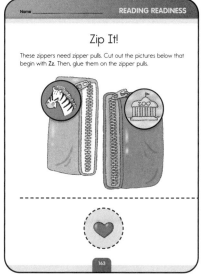

Page 163

Page 169

ANSWER KEY

Page 170

Page 171

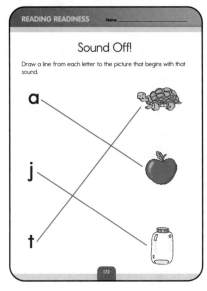

Page 172

Page 173

Page 174

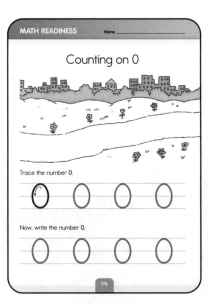

Page 176

Page 177

Page 178

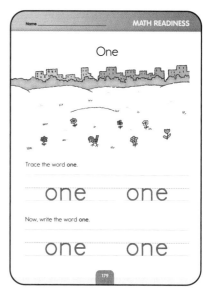

Page 179

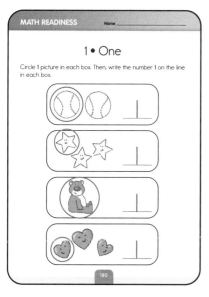

Page 180

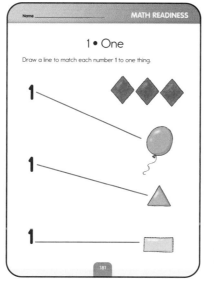

Page 181

Page 182

Name _____   MATH READINESS

Two

Trace the word **two**.

two   two

Now, write the word **two**.

two   two

183

Page 183

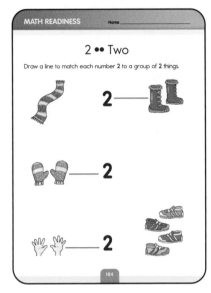

MATH READINESS   Name _____

2 •• Two

Draw a line to match each number **2** to a group of **2** things.

2 ——→
2 ——
2 ——

184

Page 184

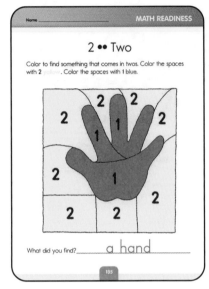

Name _____   MATH READINESS

2 •• Two

Color to find something that comes in twos. Color the spaces with **2** _____. Color the spaces with **1** blue.

What did you find? _____ a hand

185

Page 185

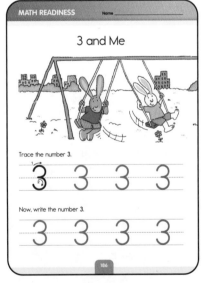

MATH READINESS   Name _____

3 and Me

Trace the number **3**.

3 3 3 3

Now, write the number **3**.

3 3 3 3

186

Page 186

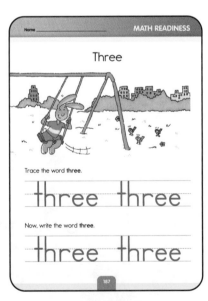

Name _____   MATH READINESS

Three

Trace the word **three**.

three   three

Now, write the word **three**.

three   three

187

Page 187

MATH READINESS   Name _____

3 ••• Three

Draw shapes that complete each pattern of **3**.

188

Page 188

Page 189

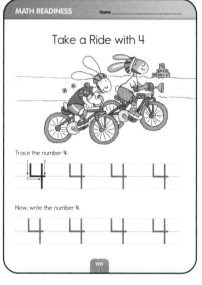

Page 190

Page 191

Page 192

Page 193

Page 194

Page 195

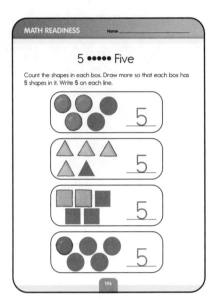

Page 196

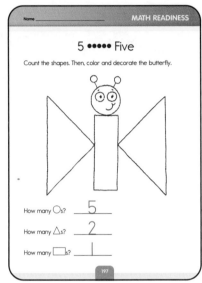

Page 197

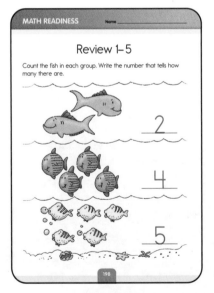

Page 198

Page 199

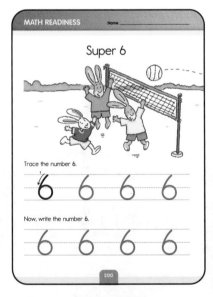

Page 200

Page 201

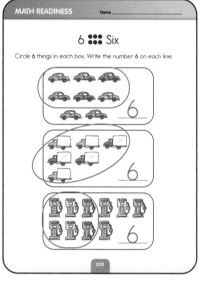

Page 202

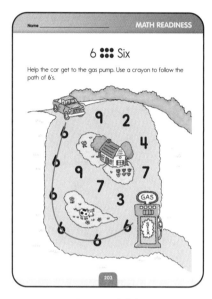

Page 203

Page 204

Page 205

Page 206

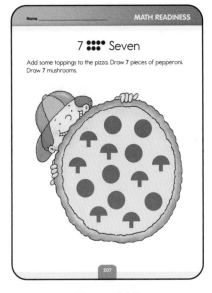

Page 207

Page 208

Page 209

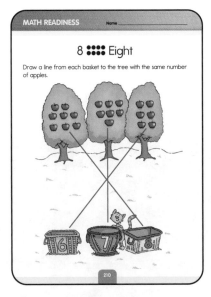

Page 210

Page 211

Page 212

ANSWER KEY

Page 213

Page 214

Page 215

Page 216

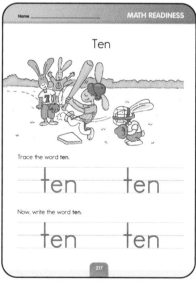

Page 217

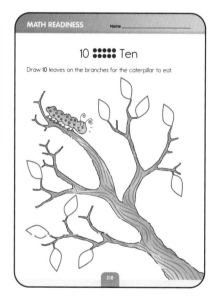

Page 218

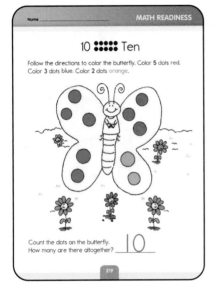

Page 219

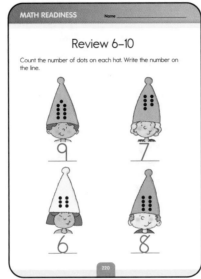

Page 220

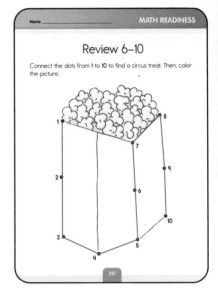

Page 221

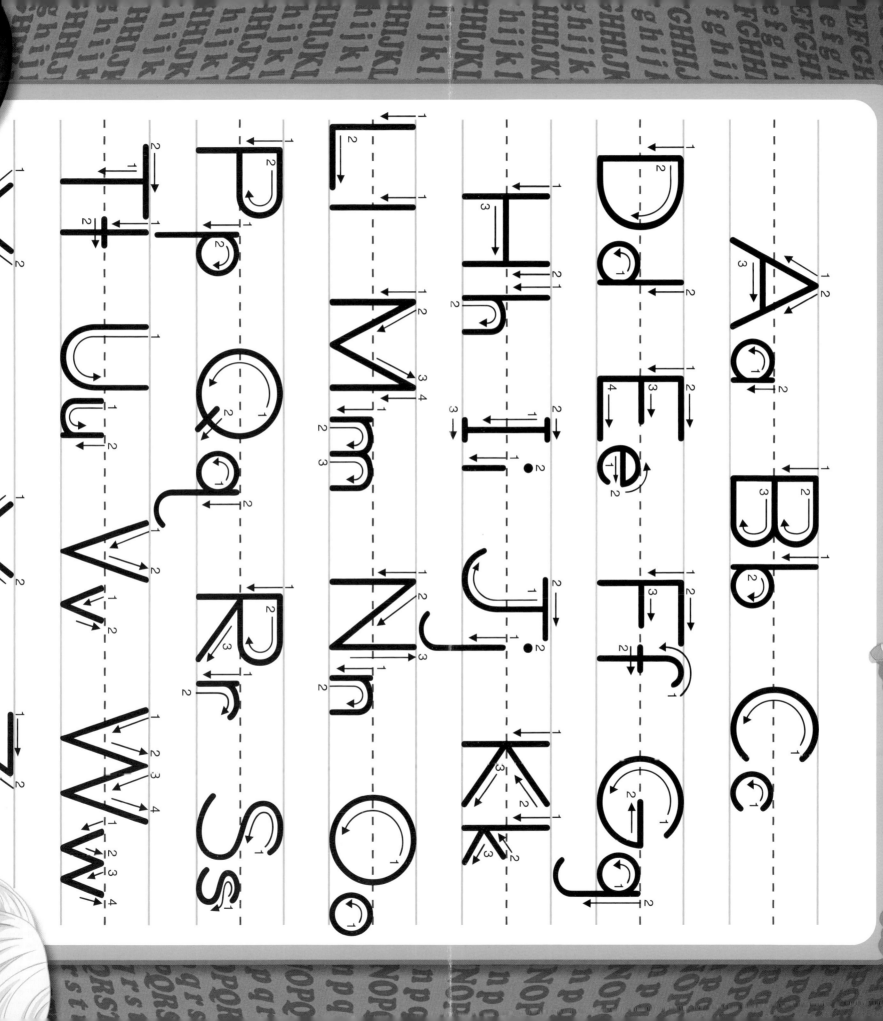

Alphabet